ATARAXIA

The Lucid Happiness

Second Edition

By Marcus Conter

"We cannot live better than in seeking to become better."

—<u>Socrates</u>

Table of Contents

INTRODUCTION

Since the beginning of our existence we, human beings, have tried to understand the mechanisms and the forces that drive natural phenomena and ourselves, our own emotions, our intellect, and our conscience. These efforts reached an amazing degree of maturity with the ancient Greeks, who laid the foundations of modern science and its several subdivisions, using rational thinking to analyze and explain the world and freeing themselves, at least the most instructed among them, from superstitious and supernatural explanations with a level of lucidity that is difficult to be found even today if we consider the ensemble of the world's population.

Their virtuosity gave us the modern world as we know it, with all its comforts and technological advancements. But, curiously and unfortunately, one of the most fundamental and important aspects of their knowledge was relegated and highly subverted over time: the use of our rationality, in a practical and conscious way, for the attainment of happiness and virtue in our daily life,

The Stoic school of philosophy, founded by Zeno of Citium, one of Socrates's disciples, was one of the most eminent philosophical schools of its time—from its beginnings in Greece, then in Rome—being very influential at the pinnacle of the latter's glory. However, only fragments of the Stoics' teachings regarding their practical advice for the attainment of true wisdom survived, mainly through the works of Epictetus, the slave philosopher; Seneca the younger; and the Roman emperor Marcus Aurelius.

Their insights are of extreme cleverness and utility in helping us in dealing with our daily problems and worries, and from some concepts developed by them we can infer some extremely useful advice in order to help us achieve true happiness, the straight and calm state of mind of the wise, which Epicurus (who was not a Stoic but whose concept of happiness is very convenient and used by them) called **"Ataraxia"** (Tranquility): a lucid state of robust tranquility, characterized by ongoing freedom from distress and worry.

The attainment of **Ataraxia** requires that <u>reason</u> (lucidity implies rationality) free us from the disturbances of passion (desires), these disturbances being the ultimate cause of distress and worries (suffering). The Pyrrhonians (another Greek school from the period) went a little further, saying that in order to attain "Ataraxia" one must suspend judgment based on dogmatic beliefs or anything non-evident to understand its true nature.

It is interesting to note that this concept carries substantial similarities with some eastern counterpart philosophies, more specifically to the Indian "Nirvana" concept as formulated by Buddhism, which aims to eliminate ignorance by way of understanding of dependent origination (between beings and things) and the elimination of desires, which leads, in its turn, to the attainment of the cessation of all suffering, or the state of Nirvana. An amazingly similar conclusion reached through different approaches, both of which are the main sources of inspiration of this work.

The inquisitive Greek spirit, allied to the chaotic environment of the world's first metropolis, Rome, laid the grounds for the mature development of the practical and down to earth Roman Stoicism, a philosophy of life that fits incredibly well to our modern world in order to help us in the attainment of true happiness and tranquility of mind through right reasoning. On the other hand, the Indian Buddhist awareness, derived from old schools of Indian philosophy melded with the pragmatic and focused Chinese civilization, blossoming in the profound and introspective Ch'an philosophy and practice (Best known by its Japanese name, Zen, which will be used by practicality in this book) produces an effective way to achieve profound inner peace and harmony through meditation. Both traditions, within their differences, shared a similar insight: that the suppression of ignorance and the ultimate freedom of spirit is the only path to the achievement of true understanding (wisdom) and the lucid tranquility of the sages. This book takes insights mainly from both traditions but also from several other sources and schools; scientific knowledge; and years of direct observation in an attempt to build a modern and practical approach in order to help the reader in the achievement of a truly productive, tranquil, and happy life—a life of ultimate peace, freedom, and lucidity, independent of your prior beliefs (or disbeliefs) and creeds.

...

This book is the result of years of critical reading and direct observation of facts and people's behavior, including the author's own behavior and sentiments. It is not an attempt to create an escape from our real lives, promising happiness through the divine and supernatural. Instead, it is the formulation of a down-to-earth and simple technique, aiming to consciously confront our real life as it is, reprogramming our minds to think clearly amidst turbulence through the control of our feelings and through the plain use of our own reasoning capacity in order to make good judgments and have a plain and truly happy life within modern society.

As the reader will perceive, each title in the summary above refers to different chapters, and they were organized in the form of advice not in direct accordance with the titles given to each chapter. This work was organized in this way in order to conduct the reader through the path of rational awareness in a cohesive and clear way, being coherent with its contents but, at the same time,letting the summary tabs serve as a reminder for future fast consultation.

Beginning with the analysis of what we call happiness and its relationship with a life of wisdom in the first chapter, you will be guided through the path of self-control in the three subsequent chapters, following the understanding of the mental process by which we react to events, which was probably first devised by Seneca the Younger in the first century of our era in his book "On Anger", in a simple but clever way:

Event --> Impression→ Feeling → Impulsive / Lucid Reaction

There are probably many different approaches and developments to this process, but this one goes direct to the point, and its simplicity permits the formulation of a coherent and simple strategy of self-control that we can use in our daily life today.

Each one of us, based on our past experiences and information received, perceives differently, most of the time, the same event. These different perceptions produce even more diverse sorts of feelings in each individual subject to this event since, in addition to our past experiences and information received, we possess different constitutions, genes, and characters. This process culminates in a reaction or non-reaction on our part, which depends on all of the above factors together. This reaction or non-reaction may consist of immediate, impulsive reactions ignited primarily by our feelings and emotions or more lucid and thoughtful reactions guided mostly by our reason.

Wrong perceptions, allied to uncontrolled emotions, produce disastrous reactions, often fueled by anger and bad feelings. This is the major source of conflict in our private lives and in the world as a whole. Thus, the understanding of this process and the use of a technique that permits us to master it, giving us the right understanding of events and the control over our emotions, is key to the attainment of this state of imperturbability of mind (not to be confounded by absence of feelings) called Ataraxia.

The second chapter explains the benefits of lucid meditation in slowing down the flow of thoughts, highlighting its positive impact in the process of emotional control and clear understanding of reality, proposing to readers a very powerful and effective technique based upon one of the most traditional Zen techniques.

An appeal to the plain use of reason is made in the

third chapter. It may seem pathetic to some and presumptuous to others, but the reality is that most of us (independent of their cultural level and religious beliefs or absence of beliefs), most of the time, and for several different reasons, commit frontal attacks to logic and consequently make poor judgments of events and of other people every single day. The second and third chapters may seem contradictory, since the prior asks one to slow down the flow of thoughts while the later begs the reader to think; however, this dichotomy is only apparent because clearing the mind of preconceptions and preconceived ideas and calming our emotions in reality opens the way for our right understanding of events, enabling our logical reasoning to take charge of the whole process.

Finally, the fourth chapter aims to bring a more profound understanding of ourselves and our place in the universe through contemplation in order to give the reader insight on the importance of being righteous and to connect the prior elements philosophically.

The manual at the end of this work suggests a simple and efficient program to be followed in your daily life in order to help you in the achievement of Ataraxia and true happiness.

On Happiness, Lucidity, and Serenity

We usually think of <u>happiness</u> as something directly related to our tastes and to our passions in life, ultimately dependent on the fulfillment of our desires: one may say that a travel adventure makes him happy; another is satisfied with a luxurious new car; others feel happy when awarded for a service done; and one may be satisfied only when immense riches are accumulated, or even when lust is satisfied; and so on, so that we usually say that someone who has the higher amount of desires fulfilled (usually the rich) is the happiest of all. However, when analyzing real facts, we realize that the world has plenty of examples of rich and famous personalities who are extremely unsatisfied, unhappy, and depressed and are much more psychologically miserable than us, the "average" people.

Experience shows that happiness depends much more on the impression we have of events, people, and things than on the events, people, and things themselves. It is not, though, a question of simple accumulation of joyful moments, but of how easily we feel happy. It is directly related to satisfaction, as indicated by the Stoic slave philosopher Epictetus: "Wealth consists not in having great possessions, but in having <u>few wants</u>"; we can obviously read "wealth" as "happiness." Also, our wants and desires must be compatible with our condition and capabilities in a <u>realistic</u> manner—not to imply that we must give up our dreams, but just that we should nurture right <u>expectations</u> and know the necessary steps to the achievement of these dreams, considering how our actions affect our environment and other people in our way and how beneficial (good) the course of action will be for all—including ourselves, of course.

In this sense, we have to agree with the view shared by many philosophers and different religious thinkers of the past who often define <u>happiness</u> in terms of living a <u>good life</u> rather than simply as the accumulation of individual feelings of joy and well-being produced by isolated circumstances external to ourselves: it is, in the broader sense, a <u>permanent state</u> of <u>well-being</u> directly related to our own <u>right understanding and impression of reality</u>.

To achieve this right understanding and impression

we must make good use of reason, developing our rational thinking and not accepting absolute truths thrown at us by proclaimed "leaders" or "messengers" as universal and immutable laws. Mainly, we must not delegate to them our right—I may say our obligation—to think! Questioning is key to this process: question for your own sake and for the sake of the rest of society too! As we will see throughout this, the constant questioning and reasoning leads to wisdom and goodness, inexorably. Just to give an example: A harmonious environment contributes to inner harmony; it is logical. So what would be the sense in disrupting general harmony for the sake of a transient burst of passion or emotion? If you have this passion under the control of your reason, you will refrain from that action or will change its course. This works for every simple thing in life and can be trained beginning with small steps, day by day.

Emotions, including desires and passions, are central elements of our lives. It is clear, as already noted early in our history and showed in the introduction of this book, that the main source of human misery is the loss of control over emotions and mainly over desires and passions. Some may interpret, when reading concepts such as that of Ataraxia or even of Nirvana, that our ultimate goal in life is to completely suppress these emotions and desires and that it is in this suppression that we will find eternal peace and happiness. It is a mistaken interpretation because of the simple facts that life is not worth living without passion and that emotions and desires are extremely important for our survival and development as species! We have to discern that there are constructive and destructive desires and passions and that sometimes the difference between the two is only a matter of intensity or control. Thus, we cannot be slaves of them, since uncontrolled passions lead to every sort of stupid action and destructive behavior towards others and towards ourselves.

Concluding, we do not need to choose between being people highly corrupted and misguided by desires with no principles and being perfect vegetables devoid of feelings. This is the main reason why we must exercise our reasoning: to give sense and guidance to our emotions. We are human beings, the passions and desires are part of our constitution and have an extremely important role in our development and in our quest for knowledge and happiness; however, they must be put under the strict control of reason. Otherwise, they may lead to destructive and erroneous behavior simply because these are, most of the time, selfish feelings, originated through primitive biological impulses for survival and nurtured in our species long before the development of society.

Sometimes it is difficult for us to control the impetus of some feelings when facing situations particularly delicate to us even when firmly exercising our reason. This is why I give quite similar importance to the development and control of our inner impressions through contemplation and meditation in this book. Without appealing to religious or mysterious concepts or to magical formulas, the fact is that profound meditation practice decreases our anxiety and stabilizes our emotions, increasing our concentration capacity and helping decisively in the development of a robust state of tranquility and peace of mind which, in its turn, improves our perception of the environment that surrounds us, opening the way to clear our minds of preconceptions, making room for unbiased reasoning.

This is the purpose of this book: to help you find a way to reprogram your perception and reasoning in order to autonomously achieve true inner peace and, consequently, the good life in happiness, the permanent calm state of mind that characterizes those whom the old Greek authors called the sages: **ataraxia**.

It is important to return to this concept of Ataraxia at this point (and to retain it) because it synthesizes almost perfectly the ideal state of mind we want to reach in order to have a truly happy and meaningful life: **"Ataraxia is a <u>lucid state of robust tranquility</u>, characterized by ongoing freedom from distress and worry."** As already pointed out before, lucidity requires good reasoning; going further now, good reasoning implies questioning and freedom of thinking; freedom of thinking implies the avoidance of preconceived ideas (preconceptions), of immutable laws and dogmas, and of magic formulas and drugs. This state of lucid mind, **inquisitive and free**, leads to the **right understanding** of ourselves and of our environment. Robust tranquility means permanent and **unswerving inner peace** which can be reached only if we maintain and develop our lucidity, being the freedom of distress and worry the ultimate consequences of the right understanding which arises from this state of mind.

The sages, or the people who achieve the highest

levels of Ataraxia, are humble, virtuous, unshakable, and compassionate. Their lucidity produces good judgments in almost every situation because they do not prejudge and also because they make good use of reasoning; they listen more than they speak because they realize they will always have much more to learn than to teach; they cultivate moderation, because unmeasured joyful reactions to eventual blessings (or fulfillment of passions and desires) bring the same imbalance to our minds as do exaggerated mourning for our losses or exaggerated vengeances against outrageous foes. The sages know that the positive imbalances tend to feed the negative ones; they do not fear death, since they recognize that we are all part of nature and that nature renews itself through infinite cycles. For this same reason, they feel compassion for all beings and are good and sympathetic to all, not out of fear of punishments in this life or another by a supreme being but, honestly, because of their profound understanding of our reality and of our place in the universe. Finally, they master their emotions and are completely free.

Concluding, it is important to have in mind that we are not good or bad the moment we are born, as some schools of thinking try to profess. We are, instead, extremely complex beings who are formed and influenced by the genes of entire lineages of families; who keep on receiving, processing, influencing, and being influenced by tons of external information in various forms during our entire lives; who are perfectly capable of shaping and modifying our character by ourselves, given our rational capabilities, which must, for this reason, be stimulated through the development of critical sense and logic from our early youth. Evil is ignorance, nothing else, since <u>our impressions are directly influenced by preconceptions generated by our past experiences and our misjudgments are generated by mistakes in our logical reasoning</u>.

On Self-Control

**Event --> Impression→ Feeling → impulsive / Lucid
Reaction**

It may seem contradictory to many readers, but the
first step towards good reasoning and self-control is
no reasoning at all! As already mentioned in the prior
chapter, the first step of the process in which we react
to any event (as shown in the scheme above) is the
impression we have of this event. Our impressions
appear to us instantaneously, in a glimpse, before we
have the time to make any reasonable judgment of
the event in question. This is true mainly if the event
is a dramatic one that has the power to ignite our
naturally programmed "defensive" feelings of fear
and anger, which usually lead to impulsive and
unbalanced reactions unchecked by our reason and,
generally, disastrous results. For example, a
misunderstanding can lead to anger that pushes
towards aggression in a fraction of a moment.

Here lies one of the greatest dramas of humans as

rational beings: how can we model our impressions and control our feelings if our impressions appear to us in a flash, before we have the time to think clearly? First, we have to understand that our impressions have no supernatural origin. Neither are they inevitable and immutable. It is true that they are formed deep inside ourselves, being the effect produced in our minds when we face a given event. They are a consequence of our prior knowledge about similar events we have faced in the past or learned about from other sources, and also of our genetic baggage as a natural biological response to this event. An impression will ignite an instantaneous feeling: if we interpret an event as pleasurable, we will feel relaxed. Otherwise, if we interpret it as dangerous or unknown, we will feel fear, and so on.

For example, suppose that when you were a child you were bitten by a huge dog—an injury that really hurt and left deep scars. It will be natural, in the future, as an adult, that when you encounter a similar dog on the street the first message you will receive from your brain is a danger warning. An immediate feeling of fear—or at least alarm—will follow. Similarly, if you encounter a lion in the savannah, you will receive this same warning, even if you have never been bitten by a lion in the past (you wouldn't be alive anyway). Because almost anyone knows from books and TV documentaries that lions are fierce predators. Even if we didn't have this information from books, probably our genetic baggage, which still carries information from our early ancestors in the African savannah, would urge you to run as fast as you can and climb the first tree available. Whether you do it or not depends on your reaction to your feelings and impression of the event. In a similar way, your reaction to criticism today will depend heavily on your past experience as a child and the types of familial relationships you were raised with.

At this stage, one may be wondering how we could use our reason before having impulsive reactions to events, since the process of receiving and processing information (impressions) and the consequent feeling and impulse to react in some situations occur in a flash. Logically, first we need to control our flow of thoughts and be fully attentive (present) to the event in order to suppress preconceived ideas and instincts; secondly, we have to find a way to put our feelings under control in order to stabilize our emotions, opening the way for our reason to take control of the situation instead of having impulsive reactions.

The best way to achieve this goal is through what I like to call "lucid meditation." This practice is based on an old method of meditation developed under the Soto school of Zen Buddhism. In that tradition, it is called "shikantaza," which means "nothing but" (shikan) "precisely" (da) "sitting" (za). It consists of a way to bring us awareness through sitting meditation. Through this method we will pursue three very precise objectives, which are:

1. Calm down our thinking influx, helping in freeing our minds of preconceptions, remodeling our impressions.
2. Stabilize our emotions.
3. Bring full awareness of the present moment in time and space.

This observation about the utility of slowing down our thought process in order to give room for reflection (reasoning) to take place before our emotional impulse drives us to action was also made clear by ancient Stoic philosophers, notably Epictetus, who used to claim: "Impression, wait for me a little. Let me see what you are, and what you represent."

Lucid meditation does not consist of a simple technique of relaxation (in spite of that being one of its side benefits). Nor is it a way of reaching another "dimension," nor does it have any mystical or supernatural intention or power. Instead, it is a practical and efficient method that we can use in order to be fully at the present moment suppressing our flow of thoughts and instincts, bringing full awareness of facts as they really are. If well practiced, It brings us ultimate reality and not the opposite, and our utmost goal is to actualize this full awareness in every moment of our everyday life.

Lucid Meditation Technique:

a) Choosing the Locality

Try to have a small place allocated to your meditation at home and use it every time you sit down. This place must be facing a blank wall and be calm, with minimal noise at the times you choose. While meditating, close the door and let only a dim light, such as the early light of dawn in the morning, penetrate the room,. Never let it be completely dark (lest you tend to fall asleep) nor too illuminated (lest you become more easily distracted). If possible, keep the place at a comfortable temperature between 20 and 22 degrees Celsius—not too hot (to avoid sleepiness) nor too cold (to avoid distracting yourself too much with discomfort). Try to meditate in the early morning or late at night to avoid being interrupted or distracted.

b) Material

There are several types, forms, and colors of meditation materials available on the market (you will find many in specialized yoga stores), and they really don't matter. They must be simply an instrument to help you stay straight and comfortable for a long period of time without losing focus, catching much attention, or falling asleep. Personally, I like to use a regular square mat with two cushions (a husk cushion and a support cushion) because I am not very flexible and it permits a variety of positions:

- ▢ A regular square mat, not more than two inches thick and filled with cotton batting, measuring from thirty to thirty-six inches square with neither cording nor upholstery buttons (no distractions).

- A husk cushion. These are usually filled with buckwheat husks, rice husks, or any other husk that is not too hard and that, at the same time, provides firmness. They measure about seventeen by twelve inches and are two-and-a-half inches thick.

- A good support cushion. These are usually filled with kapok, but you will find good cushions with other fillings on the market. It is important that it stays firm and does not bounce. Its measurements are similar to those of the husk cushion.

Many people prefer to use the round cushions known among Zen Buddhists as zafu.

If, for any reason, you have to sit on a chair or on the bed, no problem. You may face more difficulties in concentrating without falling asleep, but it is perfectly possible to reach deep levels of concentration in virtually any position.

c) Posture

Your posture during the lucid meditation should be one that permits your back to stay straight and your body not to lose balance without much effort. In order to do so, your buttocks must be thrust out, your chin tucked in, and your spine erect. Some positions are arguably better than others, but again it depends on each individual's constitution and flexibility.

If you produce too much saliva during meditation, try to press your head back so that you feel your collar on the back of your neck and be careful not to let your tongue drop from the upper palate, where it should rest.

If you have pain in your legs or if they fall asleep after some time, change the position of your legs or body. The sensation is caused by a pressed vein or nerve. For back pain, adjust your buttocks' positioning or change your entire position to one more comfortable to yourself. If you are falling asleep, try to count your breaths (see State of Mind section below), stretch your body, or get up and walk slowly a little bit while maintaining your concentration if you intend to return to the mat.

Below I have listed some of the most frequently used

positions but, again, do not stay attached to them nor try to put any mystical significance on them. They are only methods used to help us in the attainment of the right state of mind we are looking for, which is described later.

a) Hand Positioning

A good way to accommodate your hands is to place your left hand on your right hand, touching your thumbs very lightly, as if you had a thin sheet of paper between them. This position is used by Zen practitioners in order build good overall posture, relaxing your arms and shoulders while helping in the maintenance of your presence and avoiding your falling asleep.

b) Eyes During Meditation

Your eyes must be kept half-closed, looking towards the wall at an angle of approximatively 45 degrees, not fixing anywhere. Do not close them, and always remember: your objective is to stay woken up and alert!

c) Body Postures

c.1) Full Lotus Posture

Place your right foot over your left thigh and your left foot over your right thigh, with both knees touching the mat. Knees should be in line with one another, with the abdomen relaxed and slightly protruding. Hands rest on heels of both feet. Many advanced practitioners of meditation prefer this position because it permits good balance and body weight distribution; however, it requires some good practice and flexibility, and there are lots of people not capable of doing it. If you feel too much discomfort or pain, it may be a good idea to try one of the other postures described below.

c.2) Half Lotus Posture

Place your left foot over your right thigh and your right foot under your left thigh, with both knees touching the mat. It may be necessary to lift your buttocks a little bit, placing your cushions directly one over the other in order to place both knees on the mat to better distribute your weight and maintain a good body balance.

c.3) Quarter Lotus Posture

This is similar to half lotus posture, but you place your left foot over the right calf. Both knees touch the mat.

c.4) Burmese Posture

Uncross your legs, placing your left or right foot in front of the other with both knees always touching the mat. You may need to lift your buttocks even more here in order to keep straight and comfortable.

c.5) Japanese Posture

For the traditional Japanese posture, use only the husk cushion, placing it between your legs under the buttocks, with your knees in line with one another. If it feels more comfortable, you can place the support cushion over the husk cushion just below your buttocks in order to have more height. This position does not require flexibility, but sometimes is difficult to find the right back / buttocks positioning. Improper positioning can give us back pain after some time, requiring some adjustments. In a variant of this position, you can also open your legs, resting your knees at the corners of your mat in order to gain extra stability.

c7) Extended Japanese Posture

In this variation of the Japanese posture, place the husk cushion flat on the mat. Place your buttocks / perineum over the husk cushion, and open your legs wide, keeping your feet at the sides of the cushion. Distribute your weight between your knees and buttocks, moving the buttocks slightly backward in order to have better balance.

c8) Seated on a Chair

In a straight-backed chair, place your husk cushion under your buttocks and rest your feet firmly on the floor, shoulder-width apart.

d) State of Mind and Breathing

The state of your mind during lucid meditation should be similar to that of a soldier standing guard alone in the forest at night, knowing that at any moment someone intending to kill you will suddenly appear from nowhere: not fixing your thoughts on a single point, but having full awareness of everything around, sensing everything with your whole being in a completely alert stillness.

Your objective <u>during</u> meditation must be to attain nothing. Nothingness leads to pure potentiality, and from this point you can control your thoughts. While in meditation you will not think about your objective; otherwise you will not reach it.

In the first meditation sessions, you will concentrate only on your posture and start counting your breaths: on the in-breath you will count one; on the out-breath, two; and so on. After some sessions, at your own pace and when you can easily count this way without getting lost, you will count only your in-breath.

After some time, when you feel you can do it, stop counting at all, without attaching your mind to any kind of thoughts: let thoughts come and go naturally, as the clouds cross the sky, and you will pass from thought to no-thought to thought again continuously. This must be done calmly, naturally: do not try to stop thinking by the power of your will; it does not work, since it brings anxiety. With practice, you will increase your no-thought periods gradually, without perceiving it, increasing the benefits of the meditation practice.

e) Daily Life Actualization

The fully aware mind is the ultimate goal of lucid meditation, and we must actualize it in our everyday life in order to develop the right perception of all events. The best way to bring this state of mind to your daily life is to practice meditation daily, if possible, and to keep remembering to be always fully focused on what happens in the present moment, as you do while in meditation.

A simple technique that will help you achieve this goal is to put a rubber band around one of your fingers, preferably on the hand you use the most, keeping it there the whole day. When, absorbed in your daily activities, you see this elastic, stop and analyze where your thoughts were: in the present moment as they should be? Remembering past experiences? Preoccupied with future appointments or potential problems? Now, try to analyze what kind of sentiment these thoughts brought to you. The results can be surprising! In my first attempt I realized that, most of the time, my thoughts were in the past or in the future, rarely in the exact present moment. Also, I realized that the thoughts of the past very often brought me rancor regarding something bad that happened to me which I kept ruminating in my mind and, when thinking about the future, I usually felt very anxious. This simple finding made a huge impact on me, making me realize the importance of being present. From this point on, I perceived that I really needed to change the way my mind worked in order to escape the turmoil caused by the mixed and diffused thoughts and emotions in my everyday life.

As a last thought about the meditative practice proposed here, I would like to warn the reader to not attach too much to the meditation, either: it can become an addiction because of the state of peace and tranquility it can create. Always keep in mind that It is a means and not and end in itself, the end being the capacity to replicate this state of mind in your everyday activities.

To make right decisions, we need good judgment. To make good judgment we need to make good use of our reason. To make good use of our reason, we need to start by not relying on preconceived ideas that tarnish our thoughts and ignite wrong emotional impulses. To nurture a present, free, and open mind is crucial for good reasoning.

On Rationality and Thought Autonomy

Event --> <u>Impression</u>→ Feeling → Impulsive / <u>Lucid</u> Reaction

"Immaturity is the inability to use one's understanding without guidance from another." —Immanuel Kant

"When people submit to systems, they are handing over to them (to those who devised the systems) the right to do their thinking and choosing for them." —A.C. Grayling

Putting it plainly: every one of us is capable of thinking critically, reasoning, and debating arguments. So why should you grant others this capacity?! Always be aware that when you blindly submit yourself to a system, be it a religion, a sect, a political party, or a branch of philosophy, you are giving to the people who devised this system your right to think and to choose. Participate in those groups if you want and feel good about it, but question and analyze everything, and think by yourself, for your own sake and for the sake of the rest of society too! Avoid, with all your forces, sheepified behaviorisms and blind obedience to dogmas; otherwise you will be easily manipulated. Please, question this book too! Exercise your critical reasoning and create the habit of questioning!

"He who asks a question is a fool for a minute; he who does not remains a fool forever." —Chinese Proverb

Probably the greatest legacy left by the ancient Greek philosophers to our civilization, especially by Socrates, is the necessity of questioning, of inquiring about everything and testing the logic of arguments: about the gods, about nature, and mainly about ourselves. The Inquisitive mind is the very basis of the philosophical / scientific / political revolution brought to us by these early thinkers—a transformation that completely changed our perception of the world surrounding us and that raised the human being to a new state of awareness and development.

Before this revolution, everything that was not understandable was explained by the existence of transcendental and occult beings who controlled and manipulated nature: there was a god of thunder, another of sea, a god of fertility, and so on, explaining, this way, the existence of thunder, of storms, of changing tides, birth, and everything else. Demons were created to explain bad things and abnormal and undesirable behavior by people.

Finally, as very well observed by the British philosopher A.C. Grayling, the first religions were a kind of protoscience, or an attempt to explain the unknown and, at the point when human beings were able to explain more and more natural phenomena, this myriad of gods and transcendental beings was reduced and put far away from us, becoming more and more abstract and inconceivable.

Awareness about the importance of questioning established dogmas is recorded to have been first extended by Socrates in Greece and Mo-tse in China, both born coincidentally around 470 BC. They insisted on the importance of questioning dogmas and authority and thinking critically by ourselves. It may seem curious that they were contemporaries living in opposite parts of the world and that they shared this same fundamental philosophical view. But this is perfectly comprehensible if we analyze the changes occurring in the world during that period: cities and empires were growing fast, and with that growth came physical brutality and the suppression of freedom of thought on the part of tyrants who did not admit any kind of questioning. Both Socrates and Mo-tse devised simple, clever methods to exercise our critical thinking—methods we can use perfectly today:

Socrates developed the famous <u>Socratic method</u>, which consisted, basically, of finding inconsistencies and exceptions to a determined assumption through a series of questions in order to clarify it, leading to its refusal, acceptance, or improvement. It is a powerful, clever, and simple method which can help us in the development of our <u>critical thinking</u>.

Imagine, for example, that someone asserts a thesis: "courage is endurance of the soul." The first step is to secure this person's agreement to further premises asserting, for example, that "courage is a fine thing" and "ignorant endurance is not a fine thing." Now you can argue that these two new premises imply the contrary of the original thesis, leading to the conclusion that "courage is not endurance of the soul" and that, logically, the original thesis is false.

It is simple and efficient: break a thesis in parts, and search for inconsistencies, analyzing them separately. Once you put the pieces back together again you will be able to verify the veracity or falsity of the thesis proposed. This simple method is capable of clarifying the majority of assertions we face in our daily life. You will not believe the quantity of inconsistencies you will find in people judgments (including your own) by following these simple steps: politicians' promises and assertions, religious leaders' discourses, sales people's pitches, insurance offers, scriptures, etc.

Mo-tse believed that people are capable of changing their circumstances and directing their own lives and that they can do this by applying their senses to observing the world and judging objects and events by their causes, their functions, and their historical bases. This was the "three-prong method" that Mo-tse recommended for testing the truth or falsehood of statements.

Question all the time, impartially, with no

prejudgments! Do not confound blind faith with righteousness nor free thinking with immorality, since hedonist behaviors will more make you a slave of your desires than give you control over yourself. Likewise, lack of questioning will make you a slave of other people. Do not confound wisdom with smartness, either, since the world is full of smart people bragging about their cleverness and possessions but living miserable private lives. Wisdom, instead, requires humility and simplicity to clarify our views about the surrounding world. It is not only your right but your obligation to think, to rationalize. Reason must control your passions, not the opposite, in order to truly free your mind.

Therefore, you must create the habit of asking simple questions in every situation of your daily life: Who? Why? How? Apply the Socratic method! We do not need magic; we need reality! Why should you accept a dogma, a law, a piece of gossip, a story, this book, as an immutable truth? It is not a question of lack of respect for others' opinions but simply a question of respect for ourselves, of self-assertion, of individual and autonomous thinking!

It may seem obvious and banal to ask someone to

pose these very basic questions, but have you ever observed how many people actually do that? Do you do that in every situation? Are you aware of the absurd quantity of information that penetrates your brain every single day <u>unfiltered by rationality</u>? Even worse, do you realize how many of your actions you give full attention and proper rational judgment instead of acting conditioned by unfiltered information and by unchecked emotional impulses? Stop and rationalize! You will be perplexed!

It is unbelievable how often people deny the obvious because they are attached to an idea or ideology (I would say trapped by it) and are momentarily incapable of freeing their minds and thinking autonomously.

To Epictetus, the famous Stoic philosopher who lived in Rome in the first century of our era, **"rationality"** meant that human beings have the capacity to use "impressions" in a reflective manner, determining whether the content of these impressions is true or false through the examination of the **logical consistency or contradiction** between the fact under consideration and the beliefs that one already holds. Thus, if we do not make proper considerations, or if we rely on beliefs that do not clearly reflect the facts (and they usually do not), we fall into contradiction and tend to misjudge and misinterpret the situation in question, acting wrongly and/or disproportionately.

These "impressions" ignite emotional impulses that compel us to action. Actions based purely on irreflexive impulses are, in their great majority, wrong and misjudged because their consequences are not well assessed and also because our impressions are directly influenced by our past experiences, our beliefs, and our biological nature through DNA programming. Logically, each person has a different DNA program and has passed through different experiences during life. Therefore, as we do not live alone on this planet but indeed interact constantly with other beings dwelling in our society, we are obliged to balance our actions, taking into consideration the fact that each person's particular characteristics (which I will call "self" for simplicity) will generate different impressions to similar situations and that, since every society is composed by a myriad of "selves," we have to compromise ourselves to agreed-upon rules in order to achieve general harmony. It is important to make this observation to highlight the importance of balancing our actions against the world "external" to our hypothetical "selves," our "ego.

If we realize that our actions (or reactions) are, in first instance, strongly ignited by emotional impulses, which are, in their turn, provoked by our impressions on the subject or situation which we are facing, and that these impressions are molded by our past experiences and genetic baggage, which are intrinsic to each individual self, we can logically conclude that, in order to have a deep inner change and to be able to control our emotional impulses **we need to remodel the way we perceive the world**, which can be done by working in two different but intertwined fronts: 1) developing and exercising our rationality through inquiry and logical thinking in any aspect of our lives, and; 2) restraining our minds from preconceived ideas originated in our past experiences and emotions by focusing fully on the present moment, calming the mind down, and opening the way to clear reflection and prudent action as showed in the prior chapter.

Logical Conclusions about Common Situations in Daily Life

On Humility and Simplicity

"Wealth consists not in having great possessions, but in having <u>few wants</u>."
—Epictetus

A truly opened mind needs to be humble, necessarily. This should be obvious to everyone who thinks logically, since the real acceptance of different opinions and tastes requires that our ego is under control. Humility does not mean submission and humiliation before others but simply the acceptance that we are not perfect, that people are different, that there are situations we cannot control, and that we have something to learn from everyone. The truth is that we are all intellectually limited, the wise recognizes this fact.

In this same sense, we can logically conclude that simplicity and acceptance are other important characteristics of fulfilled and wise minds. Again, not that we are obliged to be poor and to accept everything that tyrants or bullying personalities throw at us, but it is advisable to be patient, to wait for the right moment to act, and to have the intelligence, once again, to concern ourselves with the things that we can control, concentrating fully on our present activities, accepting our actual situation with calm and courage while keeping our minds free and rational, clearing the way for change. Your life must be lived now.

On Acceptance and Control

"To stick to things we cannot control is to give up our freedom to things outside ourselves."
—Epictetus

To Epictetus, all external events are determined by fate and are thus beyond our control; we should accept whatever happens calmly and dispassionately. However, individuals are responsible for their own actions, which they can examine and control through rigorous self-discipline. According to him, suffering occurs as a result of trying to control what is uncontrollable, or from neglecting what is within our power. As part of the universal city that is the universe, it is our duty to care for all our fellow people. Those who follow these precepts will achieve happiness and peace of mind.

Divide your life into those things over which you have control and those over which you have not, and focus on the ones you can control. (You cannot change the past, for example). To cite Epictetus, who brilliantly developed on this subject in his famous Enchiridion (The Manual):

"Some things are in our control and others not. Things in our control are opinion, pursuit, desire, aversion, and, in a word, whatever are our own actions. Things not in our control are body, property, reputation, command, and, in one word, whatever are not our own actions."

"The things in our control are by nature free, unrestrained, unhindered; but those not in our control are weak, slavish, restrained, belonging to others. Remember, then, that if you suppose that things which are slavish by nature are also free, and that what belongs to others is your own, then you will be hindered. You will lament, you will be disturbed, and you will find fault both with gods and men. But if you suppose that only to be your own which is your own, and what belongs to others such as it really is, then no one will ever compel you or restrain you. Further, you will find fault with no one or accuse no one. You will do nothing against your will. No one will hurt you, you will have no enemies, and you will not be harmed."

This is fully applicable to negative feelings, such as anger and betrayal, that relate to the conduct of other people (which are not in our sphere of control): the choices and behavior of others are of ethical significance only for themselves, since these are under their sphere of control. To anyone else, including ourselves, they are externals and so of no ultimate consequence. This way, we should not be angry at anyone who takes a stupid decision, even if it affects us in some way. Pity would be a more appropriate feeling since, in the end, the one who will suffer the ultimate consequences of the act will be the agent themself.

Be resilient and concentrate yourself in the present moment doing your best to be a better person now, because the past is immutable (not under your control) and the future does not exist yet, but it will be a consequence of your actual acts.

The comprehension and application of this principle will naturally help you in building up resilience against adversities which are, generally, situations out of our sphere of control. Bear in mind for now that each event is the final and sole possible outcome resulting from an immense myriad of situations and facts in which you are inserted temporarily.

"It's not what happens to you, but how you react to it that matters."
—Epictetus

When facing an adversity, remember what was stated above and try always to use the adversity as an opportunity to learn and to be a better person.

Realistic Expectations about Life

Accepting that we cannot control everything and that we are, many times, obliged to adapt ourselves to undesirable situations external to us makes us conclude that our expectations about life must be very well assessed, too, in order for us to avoid frustrations and misbehaviors arising from our eagerness to possess and/or be whatever or whomever we want without considering others and our capacity to surmount the obstacles in the way ahead. This does not mean that you must suppress your dreams. No, on the contrary, you must have and pursue your dreams! But you must fully assess your situation and your capacity and all the necessary steps in order to achieve it. It must be the final consequence, nothing more than that, of what you love and are capable of doing the best now, because the path is the end in itself, not the opposite. If you think otherwise, you will be constantly frustrated and apt to commit ignominious acts. Think about this profoundly.

Indifference of Things and of the Unknown

Our expectations about things and events and, mainly, about the unknown—be it a position, a new friend, or our family—are one of the greatest sources of frustrations in our lives. How many times have you projected on others qualities and defects produced by your mind? How many times have you argued with a companion who did not agree or behave as you would like, even if you knew this person was different and possessed different opinions? How many times have you chastised your child or became very angry because your child did not match your idea of the ideal child—not taking into consideration the way your child really is?

It is very important that you try to abandon your

preconceived ideas and expectations about events that have not happened, about people you do not know, and about possible behaviors of people you know (or don't know), and to to eliminate the frustrations, bad feelings, and consequent unbalanced reactions you will produce about them. **Be indifferent!** Not devoid of feelings, unless you want to become a vegetable, but devoid of preconceptions and expectations and with your emotions under the strict control of your reason! Our impressions about events and people must be the most clear and impartial so that our judgment can be guided by reason instead of instinct and unbalanced emotions. Accordingly, try to always remember: things are not good or bad— they are just things! The same applies to fortune and riches: they are indifferent consequences of your acts. Be indifferent and keep your humility, even when touched by them; otherwise, you will be their slave and will tend to perform the most ignominious and perverted acts in order to preserve them, living in constant fear and paranoia.

Avoid Self-Victimization

Avoid, with all your heart, feeling victimized.

Our own victimization justifies everything and "releases us morally" to commit all types of transgression: from small "slips" and foibles in our daily lives up to the most sordid imaginable (and unimaginable) sadism and corruption in a being that has the potential to be rational. After all, if we place the blame for our material or psychological misery outside ourselves, nothing seems more natural than attacking this source of misery in a way two or three times more despicable than we imagine our "aggressor" is using against us in order to take revenge. It seems fair.

The problem is that, in the vast majority of situations, if not in all situations, our victimhood distorts the facts and makes us see ghosts where none exist and, even if they do exist, it makes us refuse to acknowledge our own direct or indirect (by omission and accommodation) contribution to its creation.

During our lives, we have certainly fallen into the temptation of transferring our failures and defeats to others on several occasions: no one likes to admit being a loser or being defeated, in whatever aspect of our lives. This requires maturity. When we reach this maturity, we still have another big step to make: the change. And that requires willpower and courage. Thus, unconsciously, we choose the easiest way: the infantile denial of our failures and the simple refusal to change. After all, if I am a victim, the one who has to change is the other, not me.

This kind of thinking can cause serious problems, dragging an individual into a depressive state of mind or, even worse, transforming a person into a sadistic psychopath, an unscrupulous evildoer simply a "crybaby" agitator whose sole purpose in life is denial—without knowing exactly what he or she is denying—as a response to the oppressors or the world that conspires against him or her. Another big problem that arises from this state of mind is that we become easily influenceable when we put ourselves in this position, and we tend to embrace the most senseless causes, the theories most devoid of logic, and the most absurd ideologies in our childish and eternal attempt at denial and refusal to accept the burden our own shortcomings.

Plan Your Future, Live Your Present

Be emotionally indifferent about your past; it does not

exist anymore, and you have not any control over it. But, yes, use it as tool for learning; otherwise you will commit the same mistakes again and again.

Plan your future, but do not cling to complex and rigid plans; otherwise you will create unnecessary anxiety that will accompany you for the rest of your life. Project your dream, write down your objectives, and trace a general and malleable plan. Store it and start working on it now, eventually taking a look at it and making corrections if necessary and desired. Planning will liberate you from the agony of feeling lost in life, however, it shouldn't create the agony of anxiety. Use it as a tool to liberate you to concentrate your efforts in the present—nothing more than that. Remember: the path must be the end in itself; otherwise you will be eternally frustrated.

Be Good and Ethical

"If the dishonest man knew the advantage of being honest, he would be honest at least out of dishonesty."
—Socrates

It may seem a banal question, but have you ever

thought about the utility of being a good person? If you think this is not a necessary question because your religion already told you to be good in obedience to some mystical being, think again! If you are not capable of arriving at the conclusion that we need to be good by your own reasoning, you are nothing more than a tamed beast. I am sorry for that.

A.C. Grayling perfectly clarified this point through his definition of ethics and morality:

"Ethics is about Ethos, about the kind of person one is, about the manner and character of one's life and activity. Its aim is to live a good life; which means: good to live and good in its impact on others. Better individuals build better communal environment in which to flourish."

"Morality is the obligations and duties, the constraints and parameters that apply in one's relationship with others."

We, humans, are social beings by nature. Historically, we need to interact: in the beginning our lives were almost exclusively concerned with protecting ourselves and procreating in order to obey our biological impulse for survival and constant expansion (it is amazing how it is still so powerful). With time, however, these social interactions grew more and more complex following the increase in the number of people in each community and the development of our self-consciousness and reasoning power, creating previously inexistent needs, emotions, and desires which required the emergence of "social laws" to regulate them in order to make it possible to harmonize these new conflicting needs and desires into a system where everyone could live.

It is obvious that throughout history this social development was never smooth. Many among us— mainly among the men, we have to admit—are much more susceptible to those primeval biological instincts than others and have immense difficulty in understanding and perceiving the changes in the world around us nowadays. Craving power over others, passions completely or partially out of control, they many times harm other people and themselves in an unconscious (or conscious but stupid) irrational way.

Life in society is much better under agreement—here the importance of morality and law. Under mutual cooperation and collective awareness, everything works much better. Once we cooperate with each other and do not harm people, the society flourishes. It is logical and rational, but often people do not reflect about it. Hence the education of our children has a central role in the future of our societies. We need to stimulate new free and rational thinkers conscious of their capacities and duties, not tamed, conditioned minds.

"People should be free to think for themselves, because they possess rights; but at the same time they should be conscious that their rights define their responsibilities to others."
—Marcus Tulius Cicero

To be good and ethical is good for us, since we can live unrestrained by fear or reactions and culpability; it is good to the people surrounding us, and it is good for the society in general. You do not need to be a hero and save the world. You do not need it to appear in the news that you are good. Instead, be honest to yourself and do your best to be agreeable, generous, honest, and fond to the people around you—your family, friends, and acquaintances—so that the world will be a much better place for all.

On Awareness —The Alpha and the Omega

"We cannot see the whole ocean that surround us but, in its smallest drop, we can perceive its entire reflex"
—Zen saying

Once you are focused in the exact present moment and truly open-minded, you will be much more conscious about what is happening around you. The habit of passive contemplation (without forethoughts) will open your eyes and naturally bring you awareness of reality and your place in it. "Lose" yourself (your ego) and let your mind perceive the surrounding universe in all its splendor.

Have you ever gazed at a clean night sky and thought about the immensity of the universe? Or taken a look at a depiction of our galaxy and imagined how small and short-lived we are? Try this exercise of contemplation: imagine our whole planet Earth seen from space, and envision how little we are compared to it, imagining where you are on the globe. Go further now and imagine our solar system and how much of it our planet represents. Now imagine our galaxy, which possesses more than 200 billion stars and solar systems. And go even further: imagine the observable universe, which possesses billions of galaxies and clusters of galaxies! How can one dare being egocentric and find oneself superior to anything or anyone amidst such extraordinary insignificance?! Be humble and open-minded, please. Not by blind obedience to dogmas but by intelligence. It will help you see the world and yourself as you really are.

Look at yourself now. Have you ever thought deeply about your origin and constitution? Answer this simple question: who (or what) were you before your grandparents were born? Nothing? In the cells of your great-grandparents? We have already eight people here, but it is not the full answer: you can go infinitely in this direction, which I will call "vertical." But also imagine that you, your parents, grandparents, and so on, were all subject to and interacted with different environments, ate different foods, interacted with different people, breathed different air, saw different things, had different friends, and passed through different experiences in life, all of them ultimately contributing to your and to your ancestors' constitutions and characters in an equally infinite "horizontal" sense. You, I, and everything around us are infinite in our constitution. Ultimately, the universe is contained in each one of us.

Analyze the events around you, and try to realize that the universe has some laws and that these laws are in favor of its own continuity through eternal recycling and evolution. Had it been otherwise, it would have already disappeared. This way, it conspires for the best possible events to happen in order to preserve its continuity and, since we are part of it and it is contained in us, it conspires to our continuity and evolution in the same way; we have only to accept this truth and act accordingly. Bear in mind that all the events of your life, as well as past events, even those that afflict you the most, must be put in this context: everything that befalls us is for our benefit, directly or indirectly. Remember: each event is the final and sole outcome possible, resulting from an immense myriad of situations and facts in which you are inserted temporarily and which were influenced by your way of life and by all the conditions you have created inside your environment.

This should not be used as an excuse for you to continue wrongdoings, since every action you make in all this context causes a reaction that afflicts the whole, including (and mainly) yourself. Instead, use it as a tool to forgive yourself and others and to "recycle" yourself for better. Do not blame the events; that is useless. Instead, remodel yourself and bring the events to your advantage, accepting and merging yourself with it.

A chain of bad events is usually caused by your reaction to the first event of the series. Do not live ruminating on your past; it will cause you anguish. And do not live expecting the future to come, since it will bring you anxiety. But be aware that reality is an infinitesimal point in time in which you are inserted right now; concentrate yourself on it.

The universe is "alive" and conscious of your existence, since you are part of it. You interact with it through your thoughts and actions, and it answers through events. It evolves continuously through testing variations (as in biological evolution), replicating the most efficient (good) results in order to form new species/races and to keep evolving. You are the ultimate result of this infinite evolutionary process. We all emerged from the universe and are part of it, and it is contained in us. Some way, our existence will never cease. The universe moves and evolves amidst a vast nothingness, and from this nothingness everything can emerge.

We are nothing amidst the vastness of the universe, but the universe is reflected in us in its entirety.

A Guide to Ataraxia

"And thou wilt give thyself relief, if thou doest every act of thy life as if it were the last."
—Marcus Aurelius

"Using reason without applying it to experience only leads to theoretical illusions."
—Immanuel Kant

Event --> Impression→ Feeling → Impulsive / Lucid Reaction

At this point, using the process depicted above and the concepts discussed throughout this book, we are able to infer four basic steps to be taken in order to put our emotions under the control of our reason, **changing our impression of events and, most important, the way we interpret and react to them:**

First: Calm down the thinking process, suppressing

preconceptions and stabilizing your emotions.

Second: Give full attention to the event in question. Be present.

Third: Use your logical reasoning to make good judgments.

Fourth: Act accordingly, using reason above instinct and passion so as to minimally disturb your tranquility and that of others.

To help you achieve these goals, I have listed below some practical suggestions in a more concise way than seen previously in this book:

Lucid Meditation

As already observed and explained in Chapter 2, the good practice of lucid meditation will help you in several ways: it will naturally stabilize your emotional impulses and will help you to focus your mind in the present moment, erasing your preconceived thoughts and consequently clarifying your impression of events. Start practicing it five minutes a day before going to work and five minutes at night before going to bed, increasing the the time once you get comfortable with it. In the beginning, it is probable that you will need between twenty-five and thirty-five minutes to reach the state of mind desired, which is perfectly natural, since our minds tend to process received information continuously. Do not give up! The results are well worth it. Always remember not to attach yourself too much to meditation, either, since the state of calmness it produces can be addictive. If it becomes an addiction, it will subvert us from our objective, which is a fulfilled, happy, and active life inside our society.

Give Full Attention to Events and People

Keep your eyes away from distractions and your mind out of digressions, and be fully attentive to what is happening around you now! This is the actualization of the state of mind described above in your daily life activities, and it's one of the most important—and difficult—objectives we should pursue: it clarifies our perception and understanding of people and events and reduces our anxiety and rancor regarding the possible future and the already-gone past.

Contemplate

Think deeply about the universe, your place in it, and your own constitution. This will bring you awareness of reality while exercising your humility. Be humble and admit our faults are necessary requirements for wisdom. Is there something more pitiable than someone childishly neglecting the obvious??? In its humility, the mind of the wise comprehends the universe; in its greatness, that of the stupid remains imprisoned.

Control Positive Imbalances

Imagine that tranquility is a straight line and that our emotions vary around it freely according to our impressions of events.

Consider the variations above the line called "positive variations," or those related to our impressions of events perceived by us as "happy or pleasurable events": a promotion received, the birth of a child, the victory of our team, etc. Consider the variations below the line as the "negative variations," or those related to "sad events": a death, a loss, being mistreated by someone, and so on. As discussed in Chapter 1, our objective must not be the obsessive pursuit of moments of "peak happiness" above the line of tranquility, since these moments are often related to a misinterpreted perception of reality and they will cause imbalances in our minds because we will want to be always in this position, a desire that generates anxiety and nurtures similar imbalances in our "negative perceptions" when a "sad event" befalls us. We will tend to have an exaggerated reaction to these events so that our "emotional life" will resemble Roller Coaster: the exaggerated positive reactions tend to feed the negative ones. Once again, we do not want to become vegetables without emotions. Rather, we want to have control over them instead of being controlled by them, reducing our suffering and the suffering of those around us.

Controlling our reactions to "positive events" will help us to better endure "negative events." Here, always remember that everything is impermanent and connected in a constant process of evolution which you are momentarily part of. Be grateful and happy for receiving blessings and gifts, but always try not to exaggerate your reactions and sentiments, and avoid extravagant showings and behaviors. It will pay off when bad things happen. The lucid meditation will help you to stay near the "tranquility line," too. Always nurture moderation and prudence, and remember: actual pleasures must not revoke future ones.

Concern Yourself to Control What You Really Can Control

Your thoughts and your actions. If events are only the ultimate consequences of chains of situations related (or not) to your past behaviors, they are not good or bad in themselves, so you should face them with indifference. You cannot change what was already done, but you can change now what will be the future outcome through your reaction to these events. Concentrate on your behavior and actions, your emotions and desires, since they are the sole things that are ultimately under your control. You cannot control other people's thoughts and behavior, but you can influence them through your example. Your body and those of other people, you cannot control either, nor your riches and property. Take care of them, but without to much attachment.

Avoid Exaggerated Expectations

Try not to create exaggerated expectations about your life and about every event in it, and mainly do not project these expectations on other people. This will produce anxiety and frustration in advance, which will produce every sort of destructive emotion, such as anger, sadness, deception, and fear. Why do you get angry when you lose your documents? Or when your children commit a mistake? Why are you jealous of a high-ranked friend? Or of a free and intelligent wife? This topic could be included in the previous one (control), but it was put separately here as a warning because of the frequency with which we tend to commit this mistake. Do not abandon your dreams, but pursue them wisely, taking into account the impact your actions will have on other people's lives and on the surrounding environment.

Avoid Labeling

When you adjectivize in someone, you are constructing the basis from which you will judge this person in the future. You are building a future preconception about the person. Thus, try to avoid adjectivizing people, mainly if based upon little information and exaggerate qualification. Avoid saying, "He is a crook," "She is stupid," and so on. Also, avoid exaggerated positive statements, too: "Wow, she is a genius!" or "He is a saint." Replace these statements with compliments for people's actions or less exaggerated expressions. Everyone has qualities and faults; acting this way will make you avoid misjudgments in future situations related to these people.

Negative Visualization Technique

Once a week, stop and imagine the most horrible things happening to you: a death of someone beloved, a bankruptcy, the loss of your house, finding yourself completely alone, suffering an accident, and so on. Try to imagine what would be a logical reaction to these events, taking into account all the concepts and contemplations discussed in this book, remembering mainly that everything is constantly changing and evolving and that you are part of all of this. Link this exercise with your contemplation practice. This is not a sadomasochistic exercise but rather a form of preparation for those events and a reminder of how fragile and impermanent everything is. It will help you to give more value to your beloved ones and to your own things and to live fully the present moment, giving full attention to it and to the people around you, without postponing your happiness indefinitely. <u>Happiness must be the way and not the end</u>.

Daily Balance

Create the habit of listing what you have done—positive and negative—during your day, mentally checking your reactions when facing daily events. What have you done in order to progress, to evolve, to help others, and to create a better environment for all? How have you reacted to the events that befell you today? Making a daily balance of your life will help you a lot in knowing how to face each situation when it presents itself <u>in the moment.</u> This practice will program your conscience to react to each event, since there are multiple situations that tend to repeat themselves during your life.

Temporary Self--Deprivation

Another good behavior to be cultivated is to deprive yourself momentarily (once a year or more) of the things that make your life comfortable: your house, mobile phone, car, electricity, etc. Camping in nature can be a good choice. It will reinforce your family ties and make you aware that, in the end, material things are not so much indispensable in your life, preparing yourself for eventual material losses.

Be Grateful and Humble

Vanity and exacerbated pride are bad not because they are a sin but because they tarnish our comprehension of ourselves, of other people, and of nature. The cultivation of gratitude helps in the maintenance of our humility, which is the most important characteristic of the wise, since it opens our minds to the world and clarifies our views of ourselves and everything else.

Be Kind and Good for the Sake of All, But Mainly of Yourself

Each action causes a reaction. If you eat too much or badly, you will become fat and will have bad health; if you do not exercise your body, you will become easily fatigued; if you perpetuate an aggression, you will receive aggression and hatred back. Be good and kind, and you will avoid bad reactions: suffering nurtures suffering; kindness nurtures kindness. The construction of a good environment is good for all, and if it is good for all, it is good for you. Never expect immediate retribution from others, it may create uneasiness and deception. Do good because you know you are contributing to the whole, of which you are part.. Be harmonious to your environment so that it will reciprocate to you.

Exercise Critical Reasoning

Nurture the habit of thinking critically and profoundly about every event and piece of information received in all of your activities. Ask yourself about the origin of gossip, its motivations, and the consequences in passing it forward. Use the Socratic method of testing arguments, and do not follow anything nor anyone blindly. You are the best judge of the consequences of your own actions. Avoid excuses, and assume responsibility for your acts, being honest, firm, and humble. Read, but read with awareness: one book read using your critical reasoning is one thousand times worthier than one thousand books read in blind acceptance.

Replace Prayer with Affirmative Statements

Stop pledging to god (or gods) or spiritual beings for blessings. Be affirmative, and assure yourself, each morning, that <u>you</u> will act in accordance to your wish of being a better person. You are the only one responsible for your acts and for changing your life, and you are the only one capable of doing it! It is so for every single person. This posture will make a huge difference in your life. As a suggestion, you can use the following affirmative sentences every morning or night in order to program your subconscious:

"Today I will have the serenity to accept the things I cannot change; the courage to change the things I can, and the wisdom to know the difference."

"Today I will face every kind of good and bad situation

and person, and I will have the capacity of keeping my tranquility and good judgment in every single moment."

"The only reality is here and now! I will give my full attention to every single moment, activity, and person I face today."

"I am aware of and accept the fact that everything is impermanent, that nature renews itself continuously, and that I can lose anything I love at any moment."

"Today I will carefully examine any information received without preconceptions and using my logical reasoning at its fullest."

"Every obstacle, for me, is an opportunity to learn and grow, which makes me stronger."

"The universe is contained in me, and I will act in harmony with it through my relationship with the surrounding environment and people."

You can use these suggestions as guidelines and create your own personalized affirmative sentences adapted to your routine and personality.

On Freedom, Virtue, and Happiness

Only those who make full use of reason are really free and able to fully act in virtue; happiness without wisdom is nothing more than a transient burst of joyful delusion

A Brief History of Stoicism and Zen

This book is not about Stoicism, nor about Zen Buddhism, but it's built on their shoulders. As already stated, it gets most (not all) of its teachings and insights from these schools, so it wouldn't be fair not to introduce them to the reader.

Stoicism

From the Internet Encyclopedia of Philosophy: "**Stoicism** was founded in Athens by Zeno of Citium (modern day Cyprus) in 300 BCE. It was influenced by Socrates and the Cynics, and it engaged in vigorous debates with the Skeptics, the Academics, and the Epicureans. The name comes from the Stoa Poikile, or painted porch, an open market in Athens where the original Stoics used to meet and teach philosophy. Stoicism moved to Rome, where it flourished during the period of the Empire, alternately being persecuted by emperors who disliked it (for example, Vespasian and Domitian) and openly embraced by emperors who attempted to live by it (most prominently Marcus Aurelius). It influenced Christianity as well as a number of major philosophical figures throughout the ages (for example Thomas More, Descartes, Spinoza), and in the early twenty-first century saw a revival as a practical philosophy associated with cognitive behavioral therapy and similar approaches. Stoicism is a type of eudaimonic virtue ethics, asserting that the practice of virtue is both necessary and sufficient to achieve happiness (in the eudaimonic sense). However, the Stoics also recognized the existence of "indifferents" (to eudaimonia) that could nevertheless be preferred (for example, health, wealth, education) or dispreferred (for example, sickness, poverty, ignorance), because they had (respectively, positive or negative) planning value with respect to the ability to practice virtue. Stoicism was very much a philosophy meant to be applied to everyday living, focused on ethics (understood as the study of how to live one's life), which was in turn informed by what the Stoics called "physics" (nowadays, a combination of natural science and metaphysics) and what they called "logic" (a combination of modern logic, epistemology, philosophy of language, and cognitive science)."

The site Stoic Journey divides the period of formation

and maturation of Stoicism into three different phases:

"1. Early Stoa (300–100 BCE): Zeno, Cleanthes, and Chrysippus

...Zeno opposed the popular school of epicurism, founded by Epicurus, who believed in a materialistic world and an accidental nature, driven by pain and pleasure. Zeno developed his school of Stoicism from (amongst others) the ideas of Cynicism, which prioritize virtue and simplicity. He started his teaching in the Stoa Poikile (the Painted Porch) in the center of Athens. This stoa was a covered colonnade, publicly accessible, and inspired the name of his philosophy: Stoicism. Zeno lay the foundation of Stoicism and had an enormous influence in the school. He maintained a distinction of Stoic philosophy in three areas: logic, physics, and ethics. Today, most emphasis is on ethics, even though Zeno would argue that ethics must always be supported by physics and logic.

Zeno was succeeded by his pupil Cleanthes, who mostly followed the teachings of Zeno and added little of his own. The third leader (scholarch) of the Stoic school was Chrysippus of Soli. He greatly developed the three parts of the philosophy, most notably by developing a system of propositional logic. By expanding and solidifying the foundations that Zeno lay down, Chrysippus ensured the position of Stoicism as one the strongest philosophies in history. After him, the school was subsequently led by Zeno of Tarsus, Diogenes of Babylon, and Antipater of Tarsus.

2. Middle Stoa (100 BCE–0): Panaetius, Posidonius, Cicero, and Cato

Beginning from approximately 100 BCE, the center of Stoicism started to shift from Athens to Rhodes and Rome. The seventh scholarch, Panaetius, was more flexible in his beliefs than the strict Zeno. He simplified Stoic ideas about physics and was less interested in logic. This moved the Stoic philosophy closer to neoplatonism and made it more accessible. He also introduced Stoicism to Rome. Because of the more eclectic character of the middle stoa, along with differences in opinion, Panaetius is considered to be the last scholarch. There no longer was a unified and undisputed school of Stoicism, but the Stoic philosophy would prove to be able to withstand the test of time.

Posidonius reinforced the ideas of Panaetius and moved even closer to Plato and Aristotle (and could even be considered to be a neoplatonist). In Rome,

Cicero and Cato the Younger adopted Stoicism. Especially Cato, known for his uncompromising moral integrity and his austere way of life, may be considered as a symbol of Stoicism. He seems more closely associated with the traditionalist teachings of Zeno and Chrysippus than with the eclectic philosophy of Panaetius and Posidonius.

3. Late Stoa (0–200 CE): Seneca, Epictetus and Aurelius

In the Roman imperial period, the primary area of interest for Stoic philosophers was ethics. Logic and physics were not studied as much anymore. The late stoa is the best-known period of Stoicism, since it is the only period from which full original writings have survived. One of these writings is from Seneca, who used specific day-to-day events to discuss moral issues in his Epistulae Morales ad Lucilium (moral letters to Lucilius). He is widely praised for his personal style of writing, and his Epistulae are still read today. Another Stoic author, Epictetus, is known for his Discourses and The Enchiridion (handbook), which were published by his pupil, Arrian. While Epictetus was born in slavery, perhaps the most famous Stoic was the Roman emperor Marcus Aurelius. His most prominent work is Ta eis heauton

(To himself), which he originally wrote as a personal journal during his military campaign in Germania. It is now commonly known as <u>Meditations</u>. <u>Meditations</u> is probably the most read and discussed Stoic work, and it still inspires people around the world today. Notions like self-discipline, reason, and world citizenship are still relevant concepts in our modern world. Aurelius's <u>Meditations</u> is also used as a source for personal improvement and growth and has aroused renewed interest over the last years. It is considered to be the last major work of the late stoa."

Zen

According to the BBC's website, "**Zen Buddhism** is a mixture of Indian Mahayana Buddhism and Taoism. It began in China, spread to Korea and Japan, and became very popular in the West from the mid twentieth century. The essence of Zen is attempting to understand the meaning of life directly, without being misled by logical thought or language. Zen techniques are compatible with other faiths and are often used, for example, by Christians seeking a mystical understanding of their faith. Zen often seems paradoxical—it requires an intense discipline which, when practised properly, results in total spontaneity and ultimate freedom. This natural spontaneity should not be confused with impulsiveness. The word Zen is the way the Chinese word Ch'an is pronounced in Japan. Ch'an is the Chinese pronunciation of the Sanskrit word Dhyana, which means (more or less) meditation."

The website of the International Zen Association presents a good brief history of Zen. According to it, "Buddhism arrived in China (from India) at the beginning of our era (sixth century), in a country which was already culturally rich. Two major schools of thought had flourished there for hundreds of years: Taoism and Confucianism. During its time in China, Buddha's message became immersed in the culture of this great country while keeping its own authenticity. To understand Soto Zen (one of the most popular Japanese branches) today, it is worth going back to its source and studying one of the richest periods of Buddhism: the spread of Ch'an in China from the sixth to the thirteenth century. This period of seven centuries can be divided into three great periods.

The First Period (sixth through seventh century)
From the sixth to the seventh century Ch'an developed in China after the arrival of the Indian

monk, Bodhidharma. This period, where legend and history merge, was the time of the founding patriarchs: Bodhidharma, Eka, Sôsan, Dôshin and Kônin and, the high point of the era, the sixth patriarch, Daikan Enô. Enô had two main successors: Nangaku Ejo and Seigen Gyoshi, who were the founders of two great lineages that subsequently appeared.

Second Period (seventh through tenth century), the Golden Age of Ch'an

From the seventh to the tenth century, many lineages proliferated in the transmission of Ch'an. Many of them died out, but others were to be the source of five great schools that would appear later. At the time of Hyakujo (ninth century) the first monasteries appeared with their own rules. Dôshin had already established the basis of the first rule; Hyakujo followed in his footsteps and instituted the famous rule: "A day without work is a day without eating." This was the birth of samu. During this period, the first founding texts of Soto Zen were written, such as the Sandokai and the Hokyo Zanmai. It was a time of extraordinary creativity, and reputable masters from various lineages, such as Nangaku, Sekito, Tokusan, Basô, Yakusan, Tôzan, Hyakujô, Seppô, Rinzai, Nansen, and Joshu all developed original, uniquely formulated teachings. For example, Tôzan and Sôzan, considered as the founders of the Soto School, created a large number of formulas, such as the five ranks (go i), the three paths, the three falls, the three flights, etc. All these different expressions and formulas were meant to help disciples avoid the pitfalls of intellectual understanding and get them out of the rut of their previously held knowledge, awakening them to the reality of the Buddha-way. Some of these masters were at the head of very large communities, sometimes comprising more than a thousand monks, and had a large number of Dharma (doctrine, universal truth) successors. This was how Seppô was able to transmit to fifty of his disciples. This period is called the Golden Age of Ch'an; it was at this time that the five schools or five houses came into being: Hôgen, Ummon, Igyô, Sôtô and Rinzai. Stories and anecdotes about the patriarchs of these schools have become reference points for students and are the source of what would later be called koans or public cases.

The Third Period (tenth through thirteenth century)
It was in this particularly rich and prolific context that the third period of expansion of Ch'an began (the

Song dynasty). It saw the appearance of literature which was more and more sophisticated and schools which established their uniqueness with such rigour that the cures themselves produced new diseases. Thus it was in the twelfth century that the famous polemic (true–false) took place between Wanshi Shogaku, in the Soto lineage and Daie Sôkô, who wrote the Hekiganroku, a collection of commentaries on koans in the Rinzai lineage. Wanshi Shogaku (1091–1157) is considered as the one who reanimated a dying Soto lineage, giving back to shikantaza its true meaning. Little by little, zazen had become a tranquil practice devoid of the spirit of awakening, the monks more drowsy than meditative. So, being absorbed in an empty mental state, the monks could no longer meet the demands of daily life, especially in their relationship with lay people. It was to answer critics and to the disapproval of many masters, notably Daie Soko, that Wanshi wrote his most profound texts, such as the Mokushoka, in which the practice of shikantaza regained all of its dimension and mystery.

It was this pure shikantaza that Tendo Nyojo transmitted to the young Dôgen, who had come from Japan seeking the authentic Dharma.

Dôgen Zenji (Japan)

Around the thirteenth century, Japanese Buddhism began to thrive and was thoroughly revitalized by many exceptional reformers. One of these was Master Dôgen (1200–1253), who introduced the Sôtô (in Chinese, Caodong) branch of Zen (Ch'an) Buddhism to the country. The Way he received from his master, Nyojo (in Chinese, Rujing), was centred around shikantaza, simply sitting, zazen practiced under the guidance of a master and understood not as a gradual process of liberation from illusions, but as immediate and universal access to the awakening of the Buddha and patriarchs.

Master Dôgen is considered as one of the most profound and original thinkers that Japan has known. His major work, the <u>Shôbôgenzo</u> (<u>The Treasury of the Eye of the True Law</u>), contains ninety-five texts written at various periods in his life and for a wide public. His awakening is equally expressed in the rules he wrote for his monastic community (<u>Eihei Shingi, The Pure Rule of the Temple of Eternal Peace</u>)."

Further Reading

You will find below several works which inspired the author in his quest for calmness and happiness through the years. It is not an exhaustive list, but you will find several good sources of inspiration and savvy advice that served as sources of wisdom for this book in several different ways. I highly recommend them, even because one of my main faults is to be laconic by nature, so I may have missed several details which you may judge important.

On Stoicism

The Stoic School of Philosophy, founded by the Cypriot Zeno of Citium (334 to 262 BCE) in the early third century BCE in Athens, from whom we do not have surviving works, is the main source of wisdom used in this book. Three main classical sources, which possess incredibly wise and applicable advice, are highly recommended:

Meditations, by the Roman Emperor Marcus Aurelius

(121 to 180 CE), is a beautiful and introspective notebook that unfolds the feelings of this great Stoic philosopher and emperor.

Enchiridion (The Manual) by the philosopher Epictetus (50 to 135 CE), a martyred Greek enslaved in Rome who gained his freedom and later founded his school, is an amazing source of wisdom in a compact form. His advice, mainly on self-control, is extremely clever and always realistic, an eternal source of inspiration for philosophers and psychologists.

One later ancient author who I highly admire is Lucius Annaeus Seneca (4 BCE to 65 CE), or Seneca the Younger. His works, and mainly his letters of advice about many subjects, are soaked in Stoic wisdom and are beautifully written. His lucidity is still rare today. It's simply great.

Finally, a modern work that I really enjoyed on the subject, in which you will find good references to the works already cited above, is A Guide for the Good Life by William Braxton Irvine, a good and agreeable read.

On Zen

The Zen Buddhist philosophy is permeated with sacred passages and ritualistic procedures and this fact, together with its mysterious sayings called <u>koans</u>, makes it prone to lots of misinterpretation. In essence, it is pure and simple in its complexity.

A book that grasps this core complex simplicity in a masterful way is <u>Zen Mind, Beginner's Mind</u> by Shunryû Suzuki.

To read the works—mainly the monumental <u>Shôbôgenzo</u>—of Dôgen Zenji (1200 to 1253 CE), the founder of the Soto School of Zen, can be challenging today, so I would recommend one of the several commentaries on it that I find really enlightening: <u>Le Trésor du Zen</u> by Taisen Deshimaru.

Also, I particularly appreciated the works on Buddhist philosophy by the Vietnamese Zen monk Thich Nhat Hanh.

Other Philosophical Works

There are tons of philosophy books and authors, and

you must dig deep to find good works in respect to the subject focus of this book. Works based on great pioneers in this field I find usually very interesting, even if not my main source of inspiration. Here we have the several dialogs about Socrates written by Plato and the amazingly refreshing book on the always misinterpreted Epicurean philosophy by Lucretius, The Nature of Things.

Without a specific book but based on his greatly influential philosophy in general, Confucius is always a great inspiration, as is Mo-Tse.

The hugely influential Immanuel Kant also was a good source, mainly through his Critique of Pure Reason, along with the polemic and excellent The God Argument by the contemporary philosopher A.C. Grayling.

Made in the USA
San Bernardino, CA
18 May 2020